CAR
YOU

G000058917

TROPICAL FISH

Nick Fletcher

INTERPET PUBLISHING

AN INTERPET BOOK

© 2000 Interpet Ltd.,
Vincent Lane
Dorking RH4 3YX
United Kingdom
This reprint 2004
ISBN 1-903098-29-7

All correspondence concerning the content of this volume
should be addressed to Interpet Ltd.

CREDITS
Editor: Vera Rogers Design: Phil Clucas
Print production: Sino Publishing House Ltd., Hong Kong
Printed and bound in China

PICTURE CREDITS
Artists
Copyright of the artwork illustrations on the pages following the
artists' names is the property of Interpet Ltd.
Phil Holmes: 24, 25
Stuart Watkinson: 27, 31, 40

Photographs
The photographs featured in this book have been provided by and are
the copyright of Aqua Press, France, except for the following pages:
Geoffrey Rogers (© Interpet Publishing)
22, 23, 24-5, 26, 33, 34, 35, 36, 37, 38, 39, 40-41, 42, 43, 45, 46,
47, 49, 53(R), 59, 60, 61

Contents

Introduction

Have you ever wanted a tank of tropical fish, but were put off because someone told you it was a difficult and expensive hobby? Think again – this little book will show you how to get started, the equipment you will need, which fish to choose and how to keep them healthy. From the hundreds of possible species available, many need special care, grow too large or don't get on with their tankmates. But the 20 described here are all 'community' fish. This means they behave peacefully towards one another and will happily share the same food, temperature and water conditions. This makes them ideal for beginners.

● *Below:* *A long-finned zebra danio, selectively bred on fish farms. Extended finnage is only useful to a fish where it occurs naturally and plays a part in courtship or territorial defence, but some hobbyists find it attractive.*

Where the fish come from

Wild tropical fish are collected mainly from Asia, Africa and Central and South America. But community species will more likely have been mass-bred on commercial fish farms in Florida and the Far East. Some will show brighter colours or longer fins than their wild cousins; there are dozens of forms of Guppy alone, for example.

Scientific names

Many creatures have 'common', as well as 'scientific', names. It is easier to remember 'Guppy' than *Poecilia reticulata*, but do try to learn the scientific names, too – it makes it simpler for you and your dealer when you go to buy fish. If you ask for a 'zebra fish', dealers may not know whether you are looking for a danio, a cichlid or a catfish. But ask for *Brachydanio rerio* and they will go straight to a tank of zebra danios!

A balanced community

Bottom, middle and top swimmers

To get the best from your community fish, aim for a mix that occupies all levels in the water. That way, there is always something interesting to watch.

Most of our chosen fish species will swim in small groups or shoals in the top and middle regions of the aquarium. They include barbs, rasboras, danios, tetras and all of the livebearers.

Down below we find the *Corydoras* catfishes, dwarf cichlids and that eel-like oddity, the coolie loach, which likes to come out at night when things have quietened down.

● **Below:** *Here, all levels of the water contain something of interest. Harlequins (Rasbora heteromorpha) swim in a shoal among gouramis and clown loaches. The tall-growing and compact plant specimens complement the fish.*

Top 20 community fish

Most tropical fish hobbyists start with a 'community tank', housing colourful freshwater fishes from all corners of the world that will live happily together.

This section describes 20 favourite species. They are all quite cheap to buy and stocked by most aquatic stores.

Later, if you want to breed your fish or specialise in a particular family, such as cichlids or livebearers, you will probably want more tanks – but for now, with a single aquarium, you can learn all about your fishes' needs and how to keep them in sparkling good health.

● **Right:** *Ruby barbs* (Barbus nigrofasciatus) *are also native to Sri Lanka, but most of those you buy will have been farmed elsewhere in the Far East. Unlike the tiger barb* (Barbus tetrazona), *this species is not a fin-nipper. But it does reach 7cm (2.75in). Is your tank big enough?*

Barbs

The ruby barb *(Barbus nigrofasciatus)* grows to 6cm (2.4in). Males are a rich red, females less colourful. They come from Sri Lanka. Barbs are tropical members of the carp family, and these cheerful, shoaling fishes are always on the move. This species won't eat your plants if you offer fresh green food, such as lettuce, along with the usual flake food.

The cherry barb *(Barbus titteya)* grows to only 5cm (2in), so don't keep it with anything that might mistake it for a meal. Males are a rich cherry red, females brown with a darker brown stripe along the flanks. This species is easy to breed, but endangered in its native Sri Lanka. Buy a group of at least four, as they are happiest in their own company.

● *Left: Demand for cherry barbs* (Barbus titteya) *in the hobby will ensure they never become extinct, although their natural habitat is threatened. This is a colourful male. Fish with obvious differences between males and females are termed 'sexually dimorphic'.*

Danios

You can easily see how the zebra danio *(Brachydanio rerio)* got its name – its smart blue and gold stripes are very distinctive. Wild fish come from Eastern India, but long-finned varieties are always farm-bred. Both sexes grow to 6cm (2.4in). Males are slim and more brightly coloured than females, which get quite plump before spawning. We'll show you how to breed this easy egg-scatterer later in the book.

● *Right: Harlequins* (Rasbora heteromorpha) *mix well with similarly sized community fishes, but are happiest in a shoal of their own kind. Live foods and soft, well-conditioned water will bring out their colours.*

● *Below: Zebra danios* (Brachydanio rerio) *have been bred to produce forms with different finnage and coloration. This is the golden, short-finned form.*

Rasboras

Wait until your tank has settled down before introducing the harlequin rasbora *(Rasbora heteromorpha)*. It is one of the more delicate community fish species, but well worth keeping for its peaceful nature and distinctive markings. Originally from Southeast Asia, the harlequin grows to only 4.5cm (1.8in). Rasboras belong to the carp family (Cyprinidae), the same one as your pet goldfish.

11

Tetras

The tetras featured here all come from South America. They are popular and attractive community tropical fishes. Keep them in small shoals, rather than singly or in pairs, and they will show off their best colours.

Silver-tipped tetras *(Hasemania nana)* are not all that colourful, but the pale tips to their fins mean they stand out in your tank. They reach just 5cm (2in). Look for the adipose fin (between the dorsal and tail fins, see page 23), something all members of the Characidae family possess. Nobody is quite sure what this fin is for!

Red usually means 'stop', but the crimson line along the flank of the glowlight tetra is what makes *Hemigrammus erythrozonus* a 'must have' tank occupant. It grows to 4cm (1.6in). Buy six fish, and there's a better than 90 per cent chance of having males and females. Mixed-sex shoals show their best colours.

●*Above: This farmed variant of an old favourite, the glowlight tetra* (Hemigrammus erythrozonus) *is named 'Neon Rose' because of its deep crimson flank stripe.*

● *Above:* *The silver tips to the fins of* Hasemania nana *could have developed to distract predators towards the fins and away from the more vulnerable body or head of the fish.*

The almost transparent head and tail light tetra *(Hemigrammus ocellifer)* looks lit from within, but no freshwater fish generates its own light – this is something only deep-sea species can do. This 5cm (2in) fish can be shy unless kept in a well-planted aquarium with several others of its own kind.

● *Left:* *You can pick out the swimbladder through the almost transparent body wall of this tail light tetra* (Hemigrammus ocellifer). *This organ is more pointed in males than in female fish.*

Black fish contrast well with more colourful tank occupants, and the black phantom tetra (*Megalamphodus megalopterus*), with its high dorsal fin, is a good choice. You can buy a long-finned variety, too, but be a bit careful in your choice of tankmates. Some tropical fishes like to nibble or nip at anything that trails, including fins! Black phantom tetras grow to a maximum size of 4.5cm (1.8in), but they appear bigger because they are deep-bodied.

● *Above: Give the black phantom tetra* (Megalamphodus megalopterus) *time to settle down in the aquarium. Against a dark background and substrate it will display its best colours. Note the almost transparent adipose fin; this is a trademark of characins, the family to which this fish belongs.*

● *Above:* The aptly named neon tetra lights up your tank.

The neon tetra *(Paracheirodon innesi)* is the tropical
fish that started it all! Under aquarium lighting, this
little (4cm/1.6in) beauty seems to glow from within.
Available at pocket-money prices, neons used to cost
a small fortune until someone mastered the trick of
captive breeding. They probably won't spawn in your
community tank – but as they can live for up to 10
years, this doesn't really matter.

Another dark fish is the black neon *(Hyphessobrycon*
herbertaxelrodi). Like the other tetras described here,
it should figure late in your stocking plans. That way, the
tank water will be aged and the filter fully matured,
ready for a small shoal. At 4cm (1.6in) they need
like-sized tankmates that will not bully them.

● *Above:* A plump female black neon.

Livebearers

Livebearers do not lay eggs, but give birth to fully formed youngsters. This is nature's way of improving the survival rate. Four popular fish of this type figure in our top 20 list. They will all breed in a community tank, and if there is plenty of plant cover, some of the young may well escape being eaten by other fish and their parents. Livebearer courtship behaviour is fun to watch – males have a specially modified anal fin, called a gonopodium, which they use to mate.

Guppies *(Poecilia reticulata)* are a long way from the drab, short-finned wild form found in Central and South America. Today they are line-bred for colour and finnage, and even the females can be quite striking. Both sexes reach 6cm (2.4in), but the tails of the males can add half as much again to their total length. Pregnant females show a dark 'gravid spot'.

The sailfin molly *(Poecilia latipinna)* comes in several colour forms, including black, silver, gold and marbled. Females can reach 10cm (4in), so these fish are not suitable for smaller tanks. The sailfin molly originates from the Gulf of Mexico. Males have a very high dorsal fin used in courtship displays. These fish fare best when kept warm (25-28°C/77-82°F). They do not need salt added to the water, although they can survive a degree of salinity.

Swordtails *(Xiphophorus helleri)* are instantly recognisable, although only the males have the extension to the lower part of the tail fin. These Central American fishes can reach 12cm (4.7in) – females are larger than males. Many colour and fin forms have been developed, but buy a matched pair or strange hybrids will be born. Go for well-grown males whose swords have not fully developed. This takes several months in good specimens.

The ideal 'first' livebearer is the platy in its many colour varieties. Fins are short, so won't be nipped, and even the females (twice the size of the males) will reach only 6cm (2.5in) fully grown. *Xiphophorus maculatus,* a close relative of the swordtail, is found in the wild from Mexico into Central America. A pair will produce regular broods, but keep only the best or you will soon be crowded out with drab-looking youngsters! We show you how to breed this species later in the book.

● *Above: Even a wild male swordtail has a well-developed extension to the lower lobe of the tail fin.*

● *Left: Keep the black lyretail molly* (Poecilia latipinna) *warm, or it may develop a condition known as 'the shimmies'.*

Gouramis

Gouramis are no ordinary egglayers – they build a bubblenest, which the males guard until the tiny fry hatch. More about this breeding behaviour later. A pair of either of the species described here will do fine in a community tank, provided you take special care over water quality and never let the temperature drop below 24°C (75°F). Be careful, too, not to mix them with fin-nippers: gouramis have long, threadlike pelvic fins that can be tempting to some barbs.

With dwarf gouramis *(Colisa lalia)* it is easy to tell the sexes apart. Males have red and blue-barred flanks, while females are more silvery. Several much brighter colour forms are commercially bred. This attractive species comes from northern India and grows to just 5cm (2in). One pair will be enough for your community tank.

The pearl gourami *(Trichogaster leeri)* originates from Thailand, Malaysia, Borneo and Sumatra and reaches 10cm (4in). So only keep this species if you can give it plenty of swimming space. The sexes are coloured the same, but the male has longer, more pointed, fins.

● *Above: Pearl gouramis build bubblenests for their eggs.*

Catfish

Of the dozens of aquarium catfish species, not that many are suitable for the beginner. They either grow too big, enjoy snacking on other fish, or only become active at night. But the Corydoras family have no bad habits. They are happiest in small shoals, 'hoovering' over the tank floor in search of food.

Most popular is the bronze corydoras *(Corydoras aeneus)* from northern South America. Choose between bronze and albino (white with red eyes) forms – both grow to only 7.5cm (3in). Remember, catfish need the same good-quality food as any other fish. They are not scavengers. Provide a fine, rounded gravel floor and their whiskery barbels will not get worn down or become shortened by disease.

● *Above:* Ancistrus dolichopterus *is easy to breed.*

Bristlenose catfish *(Ancistrus species)* are real oddities. They guard their large eggs laid beneath a rock or a piece of wood décor, and the youngsters sometimes survive, even in a community tank. They need plant matter in their diet and will graze on algae, but give them meals of lettuce, peas and courgettes, too. Males have much the longer head bristles. Buy an aquarium-bred pair or you may end up with a male and female of different species.

19

Loaches

Aquarium loaches can be quarrelsome and aggressive, but the only real problem you'll have with coolie loaches *(Pangio kuhlii)* from Southeast Asia is catching them. They are very agile and tend to hide up during the day under rocks, or even part-bury themselves in the gravel. They grow to 12cm (4.7in). Coolies can easily squeeze into internal power filters unless these are properly screened off.

Cichlids

Cichlids (family Cichlidae) have a reputation for being mean and troublesome to keep, beating up any other fish that share their tank. The truth is, they are highly intelligent creatures that show fascinating brood care. It is their instinct to set up a breeding territory and guard their fry that leads to aggression. However, there are a few small or 'dwarf' cichlids that will breed peacefully in a community tank if given enough space and a cave of their own.

From West Africa, the krib *(Pelvicachromis pulcher)* grows to only 10cm (4in). Wild-caught fish are delicate, but most of those on sale will be tank-bred, and hardier. Males have pointed dorsal and anal fins, while those of females are rounded. There are several colour forms, and the shape of the tail fin and the number of black spots in the finnage varies a lot, too. Kribs are fascinating to keep, and later in this book you can find out how to spawn them.

● *Left: Few cichlids are suitable for the community tank, but the krib* (Pelvicachromis pulcher) *is deservedly an old favourite. Provide some caves as possible spawning sites.*

● *Left: Don't expect to see much of your coolie loaches* (Pangio kuhlii). *These eel-like fishes are notorious for vanishing for months on end, only to reappear when you have given them up for dead!*

Understanding your tropical fish

Scales and colour

Most of the fish you keep are protected by a coat of flexible scales, although loaches and some catfish lack these. Over the scales is a layer of mucus that helps the fish glide easily through the water and keeps parasites at bay. If this coating is damaged, the fish are at risk, so never handle them directly, and take special care when moving and netting them.

● *Above: Why is the neon tetra* (Paracheirodon innesi) *such a colourful fish? The crimson rear end of the body and seemingly luminous blue flank stripe may help in communication between shoal members, signalling a collective change of direction when a predator approaches.*

The colours we see in tropical fish come from pigment cells in the skin and scales, and the light that reflects off them. In wild fish, colour helps in camouflage against predators or prey, or is used in courtship displays. The bright colours of fish whose flesh is poisonous warn off attackers. Pigment cells expand and contract to change the colours of fish at night, before and during spawning, or when they are frightened or not feeling well.

Fins and swimming

A typical fish has sets of paired pelvic (ventral) and pectoral fins, plus a single dorsal, anal and caudal (tail) fin. The single fins act like a ship's keel, keeping the fish stable in the water; the paired fins are used for steering, while the tail fin helps propel it forward. But it is the rippling wave action of blocks of muscle that do most of this work.

Some fins are very specialised. Gouramis and angelfish have long, threadlike pelvic fins serving as extra sensory organs. Males of many species have well-developed finnage used in display. Male livebearers also use a modified anal fin in mating. Manmade varieties, such as fancy guppies, have exaggerated finnage that looks attractive to us but is of no use to the fish!

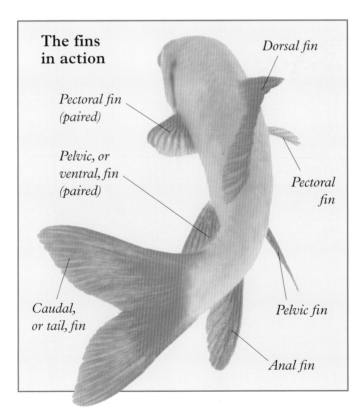

The fins in action

Dorsal fin

Pectoral fin (paired)

Pelvic, or ventral, fin (paired)

Pectoral fin

Caudal, or tail, fin

Pelvic fin

Anal fin

Swimbladder

The swimbladder, inside the body cavity, is filled with a variable amount of air so that the fish can swim at different depths with just the right degree of buoyancy. The silvery bladder also helps the fish 'hear' and maintain its balance. It is connected by nerves to small bones in the head to act as kind of amplifier. In some bottom-dwelling fishes the swimbladder is reduced, and sharks lack one altogether.

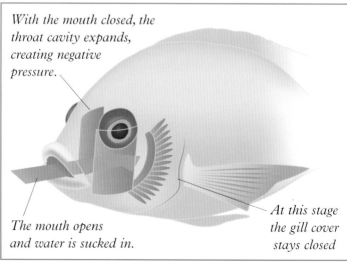

With the mouth closed, the throat cavity expands, creating negative pressure.

The mouth opens and water is sucked in.

At this stage the gill cover stays closed

Breathing

Fish breathe through gills, delicate organs either side of the head protected by the gill covers. The gills take oxygen from the surrounding water. This gas passes into the bloodstream, while the waste gas carbon dioxide, along with ammonia, is expelled. Fish known as anabantids can breathe atmospheric air directly if the water does not contain enough dissolved oxygen.

● *Left: The silvery swimbladder is a multifunctional organ. If it is damaged, the fish loses its equilibrium in the water.*

● *Below: Freshwater fishes respire ('breathe') by pumping water through the gills, which extract dissolved oxygen. This is a two-stage process, constantly repeated.*

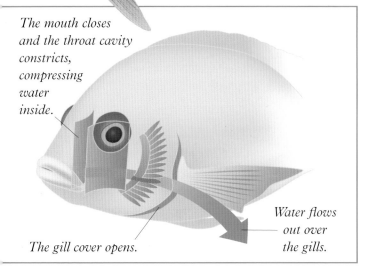

The mouth closes and the throat cavity constricts, compressing water inside.

The gill cover opens.

Water flows out over the gills.

Hearing and sight

Fish don't have ears as we know them. Instead, the tiny bones inside the head, connected to the swimbladder, team up with the 'lateral line' along the sides of the fish to detect sounds and vibrations. Some fish are blind or have reduced eyes, but can still find their way around, feed and avoid predators.

Fish don't have eyelids, but like us they can focus close up and at distance and see colours. Eyes positioned at the sides of the head give all-round general vision, even to the rear, and a binocular (three-dimensional) view forwards. Predators have excellent forward vision for hunting and grabbing prey.

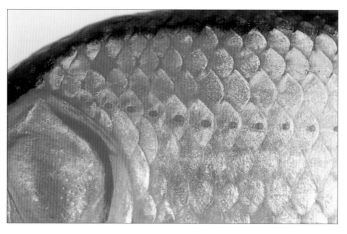

● *Above: The lateral line is a series of small pits running along the flanks, and comes closest to the human sense of hearing. It may also help detect chemical signals in the water.*

Smell and taste

Fish nostrils are U-shaped pits lined with sensory organs that 'smell' tiny particles and detect chemical signals in the water. Some fish have whiskers, or barbels, around the mouth that combine the senses of touch and taste, and further taste organs are sited inside the mouth. Often, when the water is murky, fish will locate food just by smell.

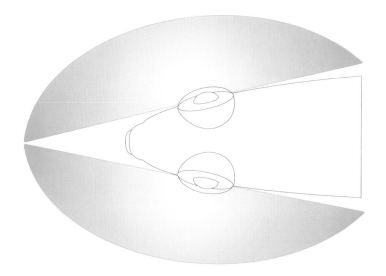

● **Above:** *The shaded area shows the field of vision of a typical fish. Objects ahead are seen more clearly than those to the side, due to the distribution of light-sensitive cells in the retina. Small food items immediately in front of the mouth cannot be seen – this is why your fish may sometimes have two or three attempts at a floating flake!*

How long will your tropical fish live?

As a general rule, the smaller species have the shortest lifespans – three to five years – although some killifish known as 'annuals' are around just long enough to spawn before their habitat dries up and they die. The tough eggs lie dormant until the rains return.

Catfish, loaches and cichlids will live 10 years or more, larger barbs up to 15. Curiously, the little neon tetra often celebrates its 10th birthday. However, no fish will live long unless it is kept properly.

Growth rate depends on good water quality, temperature, the amount of space available and the right diet from fryhood. Neglect any of these and fish will be 'stunted'. They can detect chemicals that tell them when conditions aren't ideal, and their growth then slows or stops altogether.

Questions *and* Answers

My fish are shy and huddle behind a rock. They don't come out except at feeding time, and dart back as soon as they have eaten. How can I make them tamer?

Your tank does not contain enough plants or other shelter for the fish to feel secure. Add more rocks and pieces of bogwood, and provide dense thickets of real or plastic plants so there is less open water. Once the fish know they can retreat to these if need be, they will soon become more confident and venture out into open areas.

How often should I feed my fish?

Give them as much food as they can clear up within 10-15 minutes, twice a day. One or two flakes per average-sized fish at each meal is about right. Overfeeding will only pollute the water. If you are going away for the weekend, never offer them extra rations all in one go; fasting won't harm adult fish, but overfeeding them will.

Should I put snails in my tank? I have heard they help purify the water.

Aquatic snails are a nuisance: they eat plants, and some species burrow in the gravel and multiply until they overrun the tank. They are impossible to eradicate without chemical treatments, and dead snails can quickly turn the water bad. Make sure that new plants aren't carrying snails or their eggs, which are laid in jellylike capsules.

● *Left:* Corydoras aeneus *may be friendly little fish, but they can't blink or wink at you – it just seems that way.*

My Corydoras catfish seems to wink at me. How can this be, if fish don't have eyelids?

Fish eyes can move rapidly around in their sockets, and in *Corydoras* catfishes, which have rather small eyes, this can easily be mistaken for winking or blinking.

When I come in late and turn the tank lights on, why do my fish look pale and stay close to the bottom? Are they asleep?

It's not a good idea to stress fish by suddenly switching the tank lights on in a darkened room. Fish do 'sleep', although probably not like you do. In this state their colours are not as bright as during the day, because pigment cells in the skin expand or contract in response to the amount of light falling on them.

My tank water is always clear. Why do I need to change any of it?

Clear water does not always mean clean water. Water changes dilute invisible waste products from the fish that would otherwise make them sick, or encourage algae to grow. So change 20-25% of the water weekly or fortnightly.

29

Keeping tropical fish

Setting up a community tank

Before you go ahead and buy the equipment, are you ready to take on the responsibility of keeping fish? They rely totally on you for their well-being. Tank chores take very little time, but must be done regularly. Visit your local aquarium shop and discuss your needs. Tanks come in many standard sizes, but the most popular for the beginner are 60x30x38cm (24x12x15in) or 75x30x38cm (30x15x12in). Go for the largest you can afford. You can either buy a complete 'package' with filtration, heating and lighting (probably the cheapest option), or purchase the tank and equipment separately. The second way gives you more control over the finished setup. Good aquatic dealers will help beginners like you to make the right choices. They know that fishkeeping can be a lifelong hobby and you may not stop at one tank!

Genuine dealers won't sell you any fish until your tank is at least partially 'matured' (we'll talk about that later). Tropical fish tanks bring water and electricity into close contact, so an adult should help you set yours up to make sure it's safe for you and your fish.

Finding the best position for your aquarium

Living room *A quiet corner away from doors and radiators is a good site. You will need access to electricity.*

Dining room *You'll see less of your fish, and human through-traffic could stress them.*

Hallway *Bad site, due to draughts and constant disturbance as people come and go.*

Kitchen *Bad site – heat and cooking fumes will not be appreciated by your fish.*

Conservatory *Too much light and considerable air temperature variation over a 24-hour period.*

Siting the tank

Filled tanks are heavy, and need supporting on a cabinet or a custom-made metal stand. Ordinary furniture will probably not bear their weight. If you have a wooden floor, make sure the stand rests across the joists beneath the floorboards. The tank must be close to a power point, but away from draughts and too much natural light. Avoid doorways and halls, or kitchens, where fumes might pollute the water. Quiet spots, such as corners of rooms away from windows, are ideal – the fish won't be constantly disturbed by people walking past and opening and closing doors. If you want a tank in an upstairs bedroom, check that your floor will take the weight, and remember that there may be the continuous sound of bubbling or the hum of an airpump. Noise is very noticeable at night!

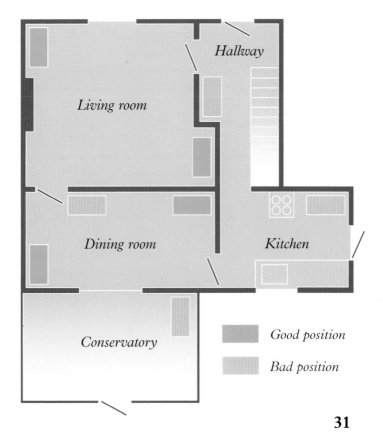

Hallway

Living room

Dining room

Kitchen

Conservatory

Good position

Bad position

Water

Treated with a conditioner and dechlorinator, most tapwater is suitable for community fish. The water should be neither too hard nor too soft, and neutral or slightly above on the pH scale, which measures acidity/alkalinity. You can buy test kits to test pH and hardness, but if your aquarium shop uses mains water from the same supply as you, the fish will be used to it.

Ideally, keep the temperature in a community tank at about 24°C (75°F). To maintain it, use a combined electric heater/thermostat, which can be adjusted a few degrees up or down. A stick-on thermometer will help you achieve and maintain the right temperature.

Why filter the water?

Community tanks need a filter running 24 hours a day, not only to keep the water clear, but to rid it of harmful ammonia and nitrite, which would otherwise poison your fish. When water is drawn through a filter, it strains out dirt particles. This is called 'mechanical' filtration. But more important is the invisible process called 'biological' filtration. Helpful bacteria (friendly bugs) make their home in the material (media) we place inside the filter and, after a while, feed on poisonous waste and turn it into harmless substances, including a useful plant fertiliser. The bugs need oxygen to do this, but your fish require oxygen, too, so keep the water moving. An airpump bubbling away will help.

What's inside a filter?

Power filters (more about these in a minute) often come complete with their own filter media. This can be open-cell foam (sponge), or special rings or tubes that give helpful bugs plenty of places to set up home. Filter wool, or floss, strains out dirt and can be replaced with new when it gets too dirty. Some filters also contain activated carbon (charcoal). This acts chemically to remove chlorine and other harmful things from tapwater. But once your filter has been up and running for a few weeks, you won't really need the carbon.

Types of filter

Filters can be air-powered or motorised. The simplest and cheapest is the box filter, which sits in a corner of the tank. An airpump draws water through the media – floss, carbon, sponge, gravel or a mixture of these.

The undergravel filter uses the material on the tank floor as the biological bed. Gravel sits on top of perforated plates, with space below, and water is drawn through it, either by an airpump or a special motor called a powerhead. Dirt is pulled down into the bed, keeping the water clean, while helpful bugs living inside it break down invisible waste.

Sponge filters run off an airpump. They provide gentle filtration and are good for tanks with young fish, because the babies can't get trapped inside.

External power filters are canisters filled with media, and sit outside the tank. An impeller motor draws in tank water through an intake pipe to pass through the media before it is pumped back, clean and purified. When servicing a filter like this, you needn't disturb the tank at all.

The internal power filter is a very good beginner's filter. This equipment comes with its own impeller motor and is attached with suckers inside the tank. The usual material inside is one or more foam cartridges, and some models introduce air into the return flow to help keep dissolved oxygen levels high.

● *Left: The main components of an internal power filter are the motor unit (top), which passes water through the media in the canister (below) and returns it in a jet to the aquarium.*

33

Making your tropical fish comfortable

Stocking levels

How many fish you can safely keep depends on two things – the volume of your tank (how much it holds), and the surface area, where oxygen enters the water. Unless your tank is an odd shape, for example very tall, allow 75 sq cm (12 sq in) of surface area to every 2.5cm (1in) of fish body length – you needn't count the tails. So for a tank measuring 60x30cm (24x12in) you could eventually keep 60cm (24in total length) of fish.

Important! For reasons you will learn later, begin with only a small number of fish and work up gradually to the total. Also remember that healthy fish grow – you must allow for this!

Tank decoration

You can decorate your tank with natural rocks, bogwood, or ornaments from the aquatic shop. Some could be air-powered, and give off bubbles into the water. Your fish will appreciate places to hide and won't mind whether you offer them a ruined castle, a sunken shipwreck or a more natural setting. Include some bogwood if you keep suckermouth catfishes. They will rasp away at it to get substances they need in their diet to aid digestion.

● **Above:** *This artificial rock outcrop is attractive and gives your fish a place to hide or rest up. It is chemically inert, so it won't affect the water.*

Never collect your own rocks or pieces of wood, because they might make the water unsafe for fish. To make your tank look natural, you can tape a plain or ornamental background sheet to the outside back panel.

Substrates

What you put on the tank floor is known as substrate.
It can be there just for decoration and to make the fish
feel comfortable, it can double as a filter bed if you
are using undergravel filtration, and you can grow
plants in it. The best gravel has rounded grains about
2-4mm (0.08-0.16in) across, and won't change the
makeup of your water. Always buy gravel from your
aquatic shop and wash it thoroughly to remove any
dust before you use it. Silver sand is a good substrate
for bottom-living fish, such as *Corydoras* catfishes and
loaches. They can burrow around in it, and it won't
wear down their whiskers. Always ask whether
artificially coloured substrates, including gravel and
smooth, glassy pebbles, are safe to use in a tank.

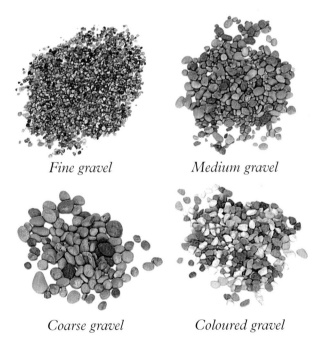

Fine gravel   *Medium gravel*

Coarse gravel   *Coloured gravel*

● ***Above:*** *Fine gravel substrates look good in small tanks.*
Medium gravel is best for filtration, while the coarser grades
are useful for large aquariums. Make sure any coloured
gravel you use won't pollute the water with dyes.

35

Lighting

Unplanted tanks are lit only so you can see your fish, but real aquatic plants need 10-12 hours of artificial light a day. Don't leave the light on any longer than that, or unwanted green algae will grow, too.

The usual light source is one or more fluorescent tubes. Some tanks are supplied with custom-built lighting, but with others you'll need to install your own inside a hood, or rest the tubes on the cover glass beneath. Each tube needs a starter unit that plugs into the mains. Ask your aquatic dealer about the best type of lighting, and get some help when you install it.

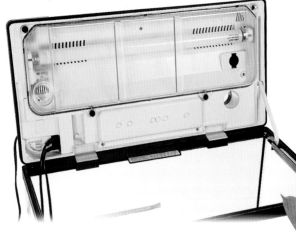

● *Above:* An aquarium hood with lighting built in behind an integral condensation tray makes for a tidy setup. Trailing cables are kept to a minimum, which looks neat and is safe.

● *Right:* Bacopa caroliniana *is easy to propagate from cuttings. It is an excellent plant for the back or middle zones of the aquarium.*

Plants

Real plants are both useful and decorative. They help to keep the water pure, hold green algae at bay, give shelter to your fish and make the tank look natural. You can't have too many plants! Some fish that need green food in their diet will nibble at the leaves, but the 20 species we have chosen will not strip them down to the stems if you feed them regularly. Aquatic plants are sold in bunches weighted down with lead strip, or else ready potted. Push loose plants into the gravel and leave them for a couple of weeks before adding the first fish, giving time for the roots to spread and anchor themselves. Plants and undergravel filters don't mix: if you have this system, containerised plants or aquatic ferns tied to bogwood with nylon thread will do better than anything rooted in the gravel. Try to mix fine-leaved and broad-leaved plants, and place the lower-growing types to the front of the tank, with taller ones to the sides and rear. Make sure that you buy true aquatic plants and not cuttings of houseplants. These cannot grow underwater and will rot away in a few weeks.

With their straplike leaves, Amazon swords make great centrepiece plants.

● **Left:** *Plant vallisneria by wrapping the roots around your middle finger and making a depression in the substrate with your index finger. Ease in the plant without covering the crown, release the roots and smooth the gravel over them.*

37

Plastic plants

Artificial plants are held firm in the gravel with a plastic anchor. They look almost as good as the real thing and will last for ages. Some look like actual plant species and are made in several sizes. Or you can choose plants in bright, fluorescent colours never found in nature – it's up to you! Lots of beginners start with artificial plants and then move on to the natural ones. A good idea is to mix the two.

● *Below: Many plastic plants are made up of stem sections that push-fit together. Vary the stem lengths, adding or subtracting sections for a natural look.*

Moneywort

Elodea

Vallisneria

● *Above: The best plastic plants mimic real species and are not gaudily coloured. These examples all anchor into the gravel by means of boat-shaped clear plastic trays.*

Foods and feeding

A quality flaked food will provide all the required nutrition for tropical fish. However, a varied diet is more interesting for them, improves their colours and brings them into breeding condition.

Prepared foods include flake, freeze-dried and frozen bloodworm, daphnia, mosquito larvae, krill and shrimp. You can buy safe live foods from your aquatic shop. Small garden worms (from chemical-free soil) are a treat, or you can can culture whiteworms, microworms, grindalworms and brineshrimp. Newly hatched brineshrimp are an ideal fry food. Some fish like fresh vegetable matter in their diet.

Freeze-dried foods: These are available in various forms and are a safe way of feeding worms and insect larvae. The small cubes shown here are made of tubifex worms and the fine dry threads are mosquito larvae, known in the hobby as bloodworm because of their colour.

Dried foods: These are available in several types, and can provide the staple diet for most fish. Offer them sparingly, as left uneaten they can quickly pollute the aquarium. Flake foods are the most common form.

Sinking granules: These benefit some of the bottom-dwelling fish.

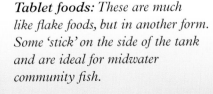

Tablet foods: These are much like flake foods, but in another form. Some 'stick' on the side of the tank and are ideal for midwater community fish.

39

Maturing the tank

It's natural to want to see fish and plants in your tank
as soon as you've set it up, but be patient – play the
waiting game and you'll avoid problems. Aquariums
need time to 'mature', in other words for the good
bacteria to set up home in the filter. Until they do,
invisible waste products won't be broken down. Instead,
they build up in the water and make your fish very sick,
or even kill them. This 'new tank syndrome' needn't
happen if you follow these guidelines:

● *Below: Planted, and
with all the equipment
running, this tank still
needs two weeks to settle
down before the first
fish are introduced.*

*The nitrogen cycle: Fish
give off harmful ammonia as
they respire, and this toxic
chemical also occurs as
organic matter (fish waste and
uneaten food) in the tank
breaks down. Beneficial
bacteria in the filter convert
ammonia into nitrite and
nitrite into nitrate, which
plants and algae take up as
fertiliser. But these bacteria
take weeks to establish. This is
why you must be patient and
build up fish stocks gradually.*

1 Leave planted tanks running for at least two weeks before you buy your first fish. This will give the water time to settle down. Real plants harbour the friendly bacteria your filter needs. Otherwise, buy a starter culture to seed the tank.

2 Start with only a quarter of the number of fish your tank will eventually hold (see page 34), adding the rest in three batches at 10-day intervals. Don't overfeed – this will only overload the filter.

3 Test the water daily during the running-in period for ammonia and nitrite (an adult will show you how to use the kits). Dilute these harmful chemicals with daily 25% partial water changes, using tapwater treated with a dechlorinator and brought up to the right temperature with boiled water from the kettle.

4 When ammonia and nitrite readings are both nil, or nearly so, the tank will be 'mature'.

Buying fish

Go with an adult to a recommended aquatic shop and stick with fish from our list of 20 – it's tempting to buy others on impulse, but then you can't be certain they will be suitable. Buy only healthy-looking fishes that hold their fins up and are free of marks and parasites. Avoid any that hide away, hang at the surface or breathe faster than the rest. Once the fish have been bagged for you, place them in a dark container and get them home as quickly as you can. Open the bags and float them for about 20 minutes in the tank, lights off, to equalise water temperatures. Then tilt the bags gently to allow the fish to swim out. For a while they will be shy, not showing their best colours and definitely not feeling like a meal. Leave them undisturbed until the following morning before giving them a few flakes.

1

Adding fish to the tank:
1 Remove outer wrappings from fish bag.
2 Place the unopened bag in the tank for a short time to calm the fish after the journey.
3 Then open the bag and roll down the neck to form a collar. Float for about 20 minutes.
4 Tilt the bag and gently release the fish.

2

3

Questions *and* Answers

How do I get water out of my tank when I'm making water changes?
For tanks with undergravel filters, use a special siphon with a rigid tube at one end. This pushes into the gravel and sucks out dirt with the waste water. Otherwise, a self-starting flexible tube with a squeeze bulb will stop you swallowing tank water if you suck on the siphon to get it flowing. Collect waste water in a bucket and use it on your lawn or to feed your houseplants.

Can I mix my goldfish with tropicals?
Fancy goldfish will live happily at 24°C (75°F), but they grow bigger than the tropical species you are keeping and may well dig around and uproot plants. They are also rather messy feeders. So, on balance, mixing them is not a very good idea.

4

Questions *and* Answers

Why can't I keep tiger barbs in my community tank? I have often seen them in shops and they don't seem to bother other fish.

Tiger barbs *(Barbus tetrazona)* will nip at long-finned fish such as guppies or gouramis. Some people say this doesn't happen if you keep a shoal of at least six, but be on the safe side and stick with the two peaceful barb species on our list.

My male guppy chases the female all day. Is this normal?

Male livebearers are always courting. To give the females a rest, it is best to keep at least three for every male so they aren't pestered every minute of the day.

How do I clean an internal power filter?

Switch off the power to the filter and unplug it. Siphon a little tank water into a bucket and move the filter into this. Gently pull off the top motor unit to reach the foam media inside the canister. Take this out and clean by squeezing it in the water taken from the tank. Never rinse the foam in tapwater or it will kill the helpful bacteria. Top up the tank, reassemble and replace the filter, switch it back on and make sure it is working properly – sometimes the impeller sticks.

Why do I need to make partial water changes?

Changing water dilutes waste products and keeps levels of nitrate low. Too much nitrate encourages algae and may slow the growth of your fish.

Safety first Before you start any work on your aquarium, turn off the electricity supply and unplug it just in case someone switches it back on by mistake. Never work on your tank with the electricity switched on.

Maintenance

Water changes

Even when the tank is mature, you'll still need to change about 20-25% of the water at least every two weeks. At the same time, siphon out solids and do other routine maintenance tasks. Top up with water of the correct temperature and add a conditioner/dechlorinator to make tapwater safe for your fish.

● *Below: This automatic water-changer uses pressure of water from the tap to siphon out waste water and replace it with fresh. Push the rigid tube into the gravel, where it sucks up deep-seated dirt particles.*

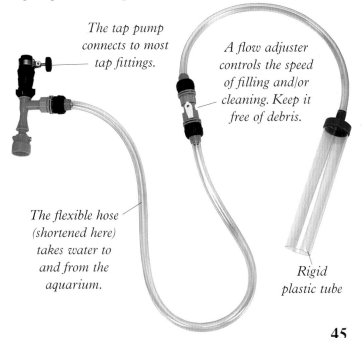

The tap pump connects to most tap fittings.

A flow adjuster controls the speed of filling and/or cleaning. Keep it free of debris.

The flexible hose (shortened here) takes water to and from the aquarium.

Rigid plastic tube

Filter maintenance

Undergravel filters won't need major maintenance for
a year or two after being set up, but when they do,
you'll have to strip down the tank and start again from
scratch. Use a rigid gravel cleaner during partial water
changes to slow the build-up of dirt in the substrate.

Box filters need their filter wool renewing when it
gets noticeably dirty. At the same time, rinse any
gravel or foam gently in tank water. Renew the
activated carbon.

Small internal power filters can block quite quickly;
you'll see the flow rate slowing down. But it only takes
a minute or two to squeeze and rinse the foam.
Replace this when it starts to lose its springy qualities.

External power filters can be isolated from the
tank with taps, then disconnected from their pipework
and carried to a bowl or bucket for cleaning. Replace
carbon and filter wool with new, rinse foam and solid
biomedia in tank water, and clean slimy algae from the
impeller. Clean the inlet and outlet pipework through
with a long bottlebrush on a flexible wire handle.

Cleaning an internal power filter

*Siphon a little tank water into a
clean, light-coloured plastic bowl.
Disconnect the power and
carefully move the filter, avoiding
drips, into the bowl. Separate the
top motor unit from the media
canister and with a soft brush
clean the impeller of slime build-
up. Remove the foam and
squeeze it gently underwater
to remove impacted dirt. Any
ceramic media can be rinsed
too, but only lightly.*

Removing algae

Algae grows on tank glass and must be cleaned away so you can see your fish. Use a double-sided algae magnet or a blade scraper just before a water change, then siphon out the loose pieces. Suckermouth catfishes will graze on algae, but you'll probably need to help them out. Fast-growing algae suggests the tank is getting too much direct sunlight, or that you are leaving the lights on too long.

● *Above: When not in use, leave your algae magnet fastened in a top corner of the front glass, ready for the next cleaning chore.*

Gently rinse the sponge. Reassemble the power filter in reverse order, put it back in the tank and check that it works when the power is restored.

47

Questions *and* Answers

My coolie loaches sometimes swim to the surface and take a big gulp of air. Why do they do this?

Coolies do not have a well-developed swimbladder. Gulping air (and sometimes expelling it at the other end!) is their way of maintaining the right degree of buoyancy in the water. It's nothing to worry about.

I have two orange platies. When they breed, will all the babies be orange, too?

Not necessarily. For this to happen, the parent fish themselves need to be 'line-bred', which often they are not. If you want your livebearers to breed true, keep only one pair per tank and buy them from a specialist dealer who knows their history.

I want to put some baby oscars in my tank – they look so cute. Will they be OK?

Oscars *(Astronotus ocellatus)* are South American cichlids that can grow to 30cm (12in) or more. Once past the baby stage, they will eat any other fish they can fit into their large mouths, so they are definitely not suitable for a community tank. Only a very few species of dwarf cichlid are.

How do I make sure I have males and females of the fish I want to keep?

In livebearers, the sexes are easy to tell apart because males have the modified anal fin, or gonopodium. Male guppies have the longer tails, while only male swordtails develop the 'sword'. In species that look very similar, males often have the longer finnage or brighter colours, while females grow plump as eggs develop inside their bodies. Failing that, buy six fish of any species and you will have a 95% chance of getting both sexes.

● *Above:* This sailfin molly (Poecilia latipinna) *is clearly a male – look at the modified anal fin. Sexing other species of tropical fish involves comparing body shape or the relative length of fins, or watching how they react with others of their kind.*

Why are some tropical fish cheap and others expensive?

The easier a fish is to breed commercially, the more the price comes down. Community species are all farm-bred, and the main cost is in shipping them overseas. Supplies of wild-caught fish are less reliable, but are of better quality than farmed fish. Specialist fishkeepers try to be the first to spawn them under aquarium conditions.

Breeding your tropical fish

Most species of community fish will spawn in the
aquarium, but you will never see the eggs or young
because they are soon eaten by the parents or their
tankmates. If you are serious about breeding your fish,
you really need a separate spawning/fry-rearing tank.
However, some community species will successfully
reproduce without this, a percentage of the youngsters
surviving if the tank is densely planted to offer them
hiding places. Livebearers give birth to quite large,
well-formed young, while suckermouth catfishes and
dwarf cichlids guard their broods and offer parental
care in the vulnerable first weeks of life.

Livebearers

Our example is the platy *(Xiphophorus maculatus).*
After mating with the male, the female drops small
(10-50) broods of live young every four to six weeks.
Depending on their tankmates, some youngsters will
escape predation, but you can improve survival rates
by separating gravid (pregnant) females into a
separate planted brood tank and letting her give birth
there. She can then be returned to the main aquarium
after one or two weeks' rest. Don't use a floating
brooding trap in the main tank. It stresses the female,
and fry retained in these traps will not grow properly.

Above: A female wagtail platy (Xiphophorus maculatus).

● *Above: Unless given a separate rearing tank, zebra danio fry will soon be eaten by their parents and tankmates.*

Egglayers

The easiest egglayer to breed is the zebra danio (*Brachydanio rerio*), but you will need a separate tank. Feed a nutritious diet, including live foods, to the community tank occupants and then set up a heated breeding tank with sponge filtration and a layer of spawning grass or glass marbles on the bottom. Fill it with water from the main tank and site it where it gets some morning sun. Choose a plump female and two slimmer, but well-marked, males. Place the trio in the spawning tank and early the following day do a partial water change using slightly cooler water than normal. This is usually enough to trigger spawning. In a swift, spiralling courtship chase, eggs are scattered by the female and fertilised by the males. The eggs fall to the bottom, out of reach of the parents. Remove the adults as soon as spawning is over. The fry hatch in two or three days, and will need feeding once their yolk sacs have been absorbed. Give them liquid fry food for egglayers or, better still, newly-hatched brineshrimp, followed by finely crumbled flake.

Cichlids

The krib *(Pelvicachromis pulcher)* is our breeding
example. Males grow bigger than females and have
longer finnage; the pelvic fins of females are club-
shaped. The community tank (the larger the better)
should contain caves – either half-flowerpots laid on
their sides or drilled coconut shells. Before spawning,
the fish will show heightened colours and 'shimmy'
to one another. The belly of the female at this time is
rounded and plum-coloured. A clutch of eggs is laid
inside the cave or under a rock, and both parents
take turns guarding these and the tiny
'wrigglers' they become. Once the fry are free-
swimming, they are led around the tank by
the adult cichlids. Although normally very
peaceful, kribs with a brood on the go can be
extremely territorial and will attack fish much
larger than themselves, so don't keep a pair in
a tank less than 90cm (36in) long.

Gouramis

Dwarf gouramis *(Colisa lalia)* need a separate
breeding tank with plenty of fine-leaved plants,
and a temperature raised to about 28°C
(82°F). If a well-conditioned pair go into
this, the male will build a deep bubblenest
reinforced with pieces of plant. The pair
embrace beneath it and the male gathers the
10-20 fertilised eggs released and blows them
up into the bubbles. This action is repeated
many times, after which you should remove
the parents and reduce the water level to about
10cm (4in). Keep the tank closely covered so
there is a layer of warm, humid air over the
water; the fry are vulnerable to chilling when
they first breathe air at the surface. They will
need very small live food organisms to start
with, called infusoria. You can buy and grow
your own cultures quite easily in a jar of water.

Health and general care

Holiday care

Adult tropical fish can be safely left for up to a fortnight with no-one feeding them. Just ask a friend or neighbour to check that the tank is running properly and that any fish that dies is removed before it can pollute the water. If you're away for longer than that, fit a programmable autofeeder over the tank or make up twists of flake into daily feed-size foil packets and store these in the fridge for your friend to give the fish. Hide the tub of flake so he or she isn't tempted to feed them extra rations!

● *Below: An autofeeder filled with flake or granules will take care of one holiday worry, but you may have to modify the cover glass so that the food can reach the water.*

● *Left: Male dwarf gouramis* (Colisa lalia) *are more colourful than the females. These bubblenest spawners are fascinating to watch. The fry need humidity and very fine first foods, neither of which can be provided in a bustling community tank.*

Health care

Even healthy tropical fish get sick if their tank is neglected, and sometimes new arrivals bring in disease and parasites, too. Most are treatable, but you have to know what to look for and catch the problem early. If you think something is wrong, first test the water – many so-called fish diseases are just a reaction to poor water quality. Here are some common tropical fish ailments and how to treat them.

White spot

Cause: Tiny parasites under the skin.
Symptoms: White peppery spots over the fins and body of the fish. Affected fish 'flick' to try and get rid of the parasites, refuse food and become lethargic, with clamped fins.
Cure: Prompt treatment with white spot medicine from any aquatic shop. Treat the whole tank.

● *Below: A classic infestation of white spot on a barb. Left untreated, this parasite is a killer, but is easily remedied if caught in time. Follow directions when using medications.*

Fin rot

Cause: Poor water quality leading to bacterial infection.

Symptoms: The tissue between fin rays is eaten away and the fins look ragged and inflamed. Fish with barbels may lose them.

Treatment: Water changes and/or a filter overhaul if the problem is caught early. You may need to back this up with a course of aquarium bactericide.

● *Above: Fin and tail erosion are signs of bacterial fin rot. Many cases will respond to improved tank husbandry; this condition suggests that you are not making enough water changes or that the filtration equipment is becoming clogged and inefficient. Sometimes, fin rot sets in after bullying and fin-nipping, in which case remove the culprits.*

55

Fungus

Cause: A break in the mucus coat, allowing fungal spores into a wound.

Symptoms: Cotton wool-like growth spreading from the wound site to the rest of the body and fins.

Treatment: Find what caused the wound in the first place (bullying by other fish? sharp rocks? parasites?) and take action. Treat the tank with a fungicide.

Visible parasites

Tropical fish very occasionally come in with fish lice, leeches or anchor worms attached to their bodies. These are easy to remove with tweezers. Afterwards, dab the site with fungicide.

● **Right:** *A serious case of fungus in an African cichlid. Don't just treat the condition; find out what allowed the fungus to take hold in the first place – often it's a wound from a parasite attack.*

56

● **Left:** *The anchor worm* (Lernaea) *and (above) the fish louse* (Argulus) *are both uncommon on tropical fish. Carefully removing visible parasites is usually all the treatment that's needed, as long as you act promptly.*

General health tips

Wounds and split fins are often caused by fin-nipping or bullying. Find the culprit and move it to another tank or return it to the aquatic shop.

When using medications, follow instructions carefully and don't over- or underdose.

Remove activated carbon from filters during medication, otherwise it may neutralise the medicine before it has a chance to work.

Sometimes, fish deaths are down to old age, so don't panic if you lose the odd specimen after a few years.

Questions *and* Answers

What do I do with my aquarium during a power cut?

Cover the tank with blankets and/or polystyrene sheets to keep warmth in. Short power failures cause few problems, but if the electricity is off for more than a couple of hours, use a battery-powered airpump to keep undergravel and box filters 'alive'. If you have gas, boil some water, fill plastic drinks bottles and place these in the tank as makeshift heaters. When power is restored, watch for signs of white spot, as chilling often brings on this problem.

One of my neon tetras has gone very thin and twisted, and its colours have faded. Will it get better?

The neon may have fish TB or pleistophora, a condition known as neon tetra disease. Neither is very infectious, but there is no cure. So net out the affected fish and end its life kindly with an overdose of veterinary anaesthetic.

I noticed after I bought it that one of my cichlids has only one eye. Will this make its life difficult?

Providing there is no infection of the socket, the fish will lead a happy, normal life with just one eye. Its other senses will make up for this; many pet fish are nicknamed 'Nelson', and now you know why.

One of my mollies has what looks like fungus around its mouth, but anti-fungus medicine isn't working. Why?

The fish almost certainly has 'mouth fungus', which is in fact a bacterial infection. Try treating it with a bactericide instead.

● ***Left:*** *Colour comparison test kits monitor the state of your aquarium. Mix a small sample of water in a tube with a chemical reagent, and after a short time hold it against a printed chart showing how much ammonia, nitrite or nitrate is present. Readings above 'zero' or 'very low' require immediate action to improve water quality.*

What is poor water quality, and how do I identify it?

Water quality can get worse slowly, through poor and irregular maintenance, or else something happens to overload the filter. Usually this is overfeeding, where uneaten food decays, or perhaps a fish dies and you don't notice. Both situations will lead to a sudden rise in ammonia levels. Sometimes the tank can be poisoned from outside, by paint fumes, air freshener or insecticides. Your fish will soon tell you if anything is wrong with their water – just learn to recognise the signals. The first job after getting a high ammonia or nitrite test reading is to carry out a large, partial water change.

MAINTENANCE CHECKLIST

It helps if you keep an aquarium log. That way, you won't accidentally skip maintenance chores. Divide these into columns in a notebook, in line with how often you need to do them. Every time you pass the tank, get into the habit of brushing your hand across the front glass to make sure the heater is working properly and hasn't stuck in the 'on' or 'off' position.

DAILY

• Remove any uneaten food
• Check the health of all your fish
• Check the temperature with the aquarium thermometer. It may be that direct sunlight through a window is making the water too warm, in which case draw the curtains or shade the tank
• Check that all the electrical items – filters, air and water pumps, lights – are working properly

● *Above: A good site for the thermometer is in a front corner, with the top just below the water surface. Check the temperature daily.*

EVERY 7-14 DAYS

• Carry out a 20-25% partial water change
• Trim back plants and remove any dead or dying leaves and stems
• Siphon solid matter from the tank bottom
• Clean the front glass to remove algae
• Wipe over cover glasses and condensation trays so that light can pass through them

MONTHLY
(Or more often if needed)

- Clean filters
- Check airstones and airlines and renew if partially blocked
- Vacuum the gravel

EVERY 6-12 MONTHS

- Service airpumps and power filter motors
- Replace lighting tubes
- Replace airstones and airline
- Clean any plastic plants of algae with a stiff brush under a running tap

(Build up a supply of essential spares, as things usually go wrong when the aquarium shop is closed! A spare airpump is number one on the list, followed by a back-up heater/thermostat).

● *Above: With regular maintenance, your tank will continue to look as good as the day you set it up (or better, because the plants and fish will have grown)!*

About my tropical fish

My favourite tropical fish is called

_____

What type? My tropical fish is a

_____

Stick a photo of your pet here

My fish's favourite plant is

_____

My fish's favourite food is

_____

My vet's name is

_____

My vet's telephone number is

_____

Index

Page numbers in *italics* refer to captions to photographs.

● *Above: A shoal of lively cardinal tetras* (Paracheirodon axelrodi) *sums up the pleasures of tropical fishkeeping. These are beautiful and responsive pets.*